Born to be Wild
Little Bears

Valérie Guidoux

Words that appear in the glossary are printed in
boldface type the first time they occur in the text.

GARETH**STEVENS**
GS
PUBLISHING
A Member of the WRC Media Family of Companies

Inside a Bear's Den

Little bears are called cubs. At birth, they are as small as rabbits and weigh only about 8 to 16 ounces (227 to 453 grams). Mother bears feed their cubs milk, and in two months, the little bears weigh almost 7 pounds (3 kilograms). Snug and warm in its **den**, a bear cub plays with its brother or sister. The cubs **growl** at each other as they climb over their mother and jump between her huge paws. Their mother sleeps with one eye open, watching her babies. Peace returns to the bears' den after the cubs fall asleep on a bed of dried grasses and moss.

A mother bear gives birth to between one and three cubs at a time. The little bears follow their mother everywhere until they are about four months old.

What do you think?

What do bears do all winter?

a) They travel.

b) They stay in their dens and nap until spring.

c) They hunt for hazelnuts and acorns.

3

In winter, there is not much food for bears to eat. They fight off hunger and cold by **hibernating**, or staying inactive. When a bear hibernates, its heart beats more slowly, and its breathing is **shallow**. The bear naps and eats nothing until spring. Each bear has his or her own spot in which to hibernate. Rolled into a ball in his hiding place, a male bear sleeps for three or four months. Alone in her den, a female bear gives birth to her babies in the middle of winter. As soon as it is warm enough to leave the den, the cubs follow their mother around until April or May, when they are about four months old.

Before winter, a bear eats as much as it can, feeding on beechnuts, hazelnuts, chestnuts, acorns, mushrooms, and other foods that ripen in fall. The bear is building stores of fat so it will be able to go without eating until March or April.

A bear's den might be a cave in the rocks, a sheltered spot between the roots of a tree, or a hole dug into a hill. The bear covers the floor of its den with grasses, moss, and leaves. It closes the entrance with branches, from the inside.

So it will not be disturbed, a bear builds its den in a place far away from people and other bears. It enters its shelter at the beginning of winter, just before the first snowfall. The snow covers the den, hiding it and protecting it from extremely cold weather.

A bear leaves its den as soon as the weather warms up and the snow begins to melt. While waiting for spring plants to grow, the bear's fat reserves help it stay alive.

Romping, Climbing, and Rolling Around

Curious and **mischievous** little bears run around in forests, dig under bushes, climb over rocks, roll in mud, and fight playfully. Their mothers let them explore and play because that is how cubs learn and grow. If a cub strays too far, however, its mother will growl at it and punish it by slapping it with her paw.

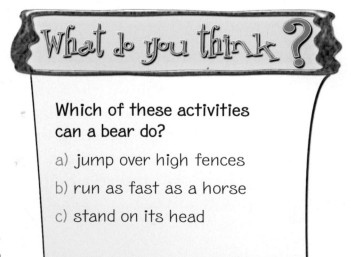

What do you think?

Which of these activities can a bear do?

a) jump over high fences

b) run as fast as a horse

c) stand on its head

Although a mother bear lets her cubs **venture** into a field or a forest, she stays close and watches over them. She never leaves her babies and will **fiercely** defend them when she thinks they are in danger.

A bear can run as fast as a horse.

Most of the time, bears walk slowly, but they can run at high speeds. Bears can run as fast as 35 miles (56 kilometers) an hour, but they cannot keep up this speed over long distances. When a bear runs, its thick coat ripples like a rug or a blanket that is being shaken. In spite of their size and clumsy appearance, bears are **agile** animals. Some bears can easily climb trees! Bear cubs climb trees to play, while adult bears climb them to catch insects and reach fruit and honey. Bears are good swimmers, too, and when the weather is warm, they often splash around in rivers.

A bear walks with the bottoms of all four feet flat on the ground. It lifts two paws at a time, first on one side of its body, then on the other side.

Cubs spend most of their time playing and often climb trees. At six months of age, they are about the size of big cats. Unlike some kinds of bears, such as black bears, adult brown bears are too big to climb trees.

A Bear-Sized Appetite

A full-grown bear spends most of its time looking for food. This large animal will eat almost anything, including a whole sheep or a baby deer or baby moose. Usually, however, a bear eats small things, such as seeds, berries, the roots of plants, and all kinds of tiny insects. To satisfy its huge appetite, a bear must eat a lot of caterpillars, hornets, wasps, grasshoppers, or ants. To catch ants, a bear uses its sharp claws to break open the ant hills or fallen logs in which ants live. When the ants crawl over the bear's paws, the bear licks them off. Bears eat other small animals, too, such as snails, frogs, ground squirrels, **voles**, and fish.

When they are five months old, bear cubs begin learning from their mothers how to hunt for food. They can feed themselves now so they stop drinking their mothers' milk.

What do you think?

What is a bear's favorite food?

a) honey

b) ants

c) milk

Honey is a bear's favorite food.

During warm weather, bears have an easy time finding enough food to eat. Both adult bears and cubs like to eat sweet foods, especially honey! Some little bears use their lips and tongues to pull sweet, ripe raspberries off bushes. Other cubs paw the ground with their claws to pull up crunchy roots. Meanwhile, with just a flick of her paw, a mother bear turns over a big rock to catch tiny ants.

A bear can destroy an entire swarm, or group, of bees trying to get honey. The bear may pay for this sweet food, however, with many painful bee stings! Sometimes, a bear has to dive into a river to escape from angry bees.

When a bear finds a large supply of food, it eats all it can. Then, with a full stomach, it might very well fall asleep right there!

A bear has special ways of catching salmon or trout. Sometimes, the bear perches on a rock in the middle of a river to look for fish. Then, with a toss of its **muzzle**, it catches a jumping fish when the fish is still in the air.

Bears are omnivores, which means they eat both plants and animals. They often eat dead animals that they find, including deer, moose, elk, and mountain goats. Sometimes, bears hunt fawns and baby elk or attack other easy **prey**, such as sheep or cows.

Staying Safe

Bears are often active at night when there is less chance they will be disturbed by dogs or by people hiking. Sometimes, a mother bear will suddenly stand up on her back feet. She can sense that another animal is coming near, and she wants to find out what it is. If the animal approaching is an adult male bear, she growls to show he is not welcome near her cubs. Her warning lets him know that she is not going to **mate** with him, and he should stay away.

What do you think?

What is the best way for bears to detect or locate danger?

a) with their eyes

b) with their senses of smell and hearing

c) with their whiskers

Although bears can stand up on two legs, they usually do it only when they want to pick up a scent or get a better look at their surroundings.

14

The best way for bears to detect danger is with their senses of smell and hearing.

Bears can see about as well as humans can, but because bears are forest animals, living among trees and bushes, they do not need to see very far.

Male and female bears live separately, and bear cubs never know their fathers. Adult bears meet only in the middle of summer to mate. They stay together for several days in the deepest part of the forest. After mating, the bears separate again. A mother bear waits until her cubs are a year old before leaving them to mate again with a male bear.

Male bears are much bigger than females. A mother bear with young cubs will not allow a male to come near the cubs because he might attack them.

Bears use gestures and other ways of moving their bodies to communicate with each other. They also grumble, groan, and cry out.

At any time, a bear may stop what it is doing, prick up its ears, and raise its muzzle to sniff the air. Bears can hear the tiniest sounds, and their long noses can pick up every smell. Any kind of animal will have difficulty getting near a bear without being noticed.

On Their Own

After two years, the time for young bears to cuddle with their mothers is over. The youngsters are left alone because they are old enough now to take care of themselves. For several days, each young bear explores a new forest or mountain slope. Winter is coming, and the young bears must find places to set up their dens. Along the way, a bear might collect mushrooms, run through a meadow, or spend a long time scratching its back against a tree.

When bear cubs are two years old, they are about the size of big dogs, and each weighs about 90 pounds (40 kg).

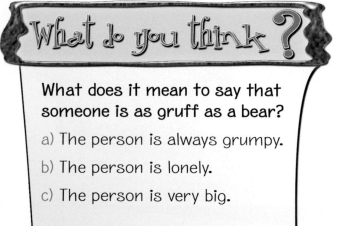

What do you think?

What does it mean to say that someone is as gruff as a bear?

a) The person is always grumpy.

b) The person is lonely.

c) The person is very big.

To say that someone is as gruff as a bear means the person is always grumpy.

Although a bear lives alone, its **home range**, or the area in which the bear hunts for food, may overlap with the home ranges of other bears. When two bears run into each other, they often growl and clack their teeth until the weaker bear runs away. Bears will fight with each other only on rare occasions, but they sometimes exchange a couple of friendly swats with their paws.

Because it is not very trusting, a bear runs away quietly as soon as it notices someone or something coming near it. Bears are usually dangerous only if they feel they are being attacked. Female bears, however, may become fierce any time they think their cubs are in danger.

Each bear marks its home range with signs that other bears can easily recognize — claw marks on a tree's bark, the bear's scent and small pieces of its fur on trees that it has rubbed against, or droppings or paw marks on the ground. These signs help each bear stay within its own home range and know when it is entering the range of another bear.

In certain regions, bears come together at rivers where there are lots of salmon or trout. The strongest bears take the best spots on the river and growl at weaker bears that dare to catch fish the strong bears think should be their own.

Male bears continue growing until they are ten years old. Females reach their full height and can give birth when they are only five years old.

21

Bears are **mammals**. Most bears live north of the **equator**, but one kind of bear lives in northern South America, on the slopes of the Andes Mountains. Brown bears are found in the mountainous areas of Europe, North America, and Asia. About 70 percent of brown bears in North America live in Alaska. The largest brown bears are the Kodiak bears that live along the Alaskan coast. Brown bears that live inland, or away from the coast, are called grizzly bears. Brown bears live about 20 to 26 years, and except for a mother with cubs, they live alone. Adult bears weigh the most in late summer and fall. During that time, male brown bears usually weigh 500 to 900 pounds (227 to 408 kg), but some weigh as much as 1,500 pounds (680 kg). Females weigh one-half to three-quarters as much as males. All kinds of bears are related to each other and to giant pandas.

When they are standing on their back legs, brown bears can be 6 to 9 feet (2 to 3 meters) tall.

Standing on four legs,
a brown bear is about
42 inches (107 centimeters)
high at its shoulders.

The strong muscles on a
brown bear's shoulders form
a hump under the bear's fur.
These muscles give the bear's
front legs extra strength.

A bear's sense of smell
is stronger than any
other animal's. A bear
uses its senses of smell
and hearing to find food
and pinpoint danger.

The claws on
a brown bear's
paws are 2 to
4 inches (5 to
10 cm) long.
A bear uses
its claws to dig
a den and to
dig for food.

GLOSSARY

agile — able to move quickly and easily

den — a cave or hollow that a wild animal uses for shelter

equator — an imaginary line that circles the middle of Earth, halfway between the North and South Poles

fiercely — violently wild

growl — to make a low sound deep in the throat

hibernating — spending winter in an inactive state such as resting or sleeping

home range — the area in which an animal sleeps and finds food and water

mammals — warm-blooded animals that have backbones, give birth to live babies, feed their young with milk from the mother's body, and have skin that is covered with hair or fur

mate — (v) to join together to produce young

mischievous — naughty in a playful way

muzzle — the front of the head of an animal, which sticks out and on which the animal's nose and mouth are located

prey — (n) animals that are hunted and killed by other animals, usually for food

shallow — not deep

venture — to take on the risks and dangers of an activity

voles — mouselike animals

Please visit our web site at: www.garethstevens.com
For a free color catalog describing Gareth Stevens Publishing's list of high-quality books and multimedia programs, call 1-800-542-2595 (USA) or 1-800-387-3178 (Canada). Gareth Stevens Publishing's fax: (414) 332-3567.

Library of Congress Cataloging-in-Publication Data

Guidoux, Valérie.
   [Petit ours. English]
   Little bears / Valérie Guidoux. — North American ed.
     p. cm. — (Born to be wild)
     ISBN-10: 0-8368-6696-7 — ISBN-13: 978-0-8368-6696-4 (lib. bdg.)
     1. Bears—Infancy—Juvenile literature. 2. Bears—Juvenile literature. I. Title. II. Series.
   QL737.C27G8413   2007
   599.74'446—dc22   2005037415

This North American edition first published in 2007 by
Gareth Stevens Publishing
A Member of the WRC Media Family of Companies
330 West Olive Street, Suite 100
Milwaukee, Wisconsin 53212 USA

First published in 2000 as *Le petit ours* by Mango Jeunesse, an imprint of Editions Mango, Paris, France. Additional end matter copyright © 2007 by Gareth Stevens, Inc.

Picture Credits (t=top, b=bottom, l=left, r=right, c=center)
Colibri: J. L. Ermel 5(t), 10; Philippe Emery 5(b); A. M. Loubsens 16(b), back cover. Jacana: Étienne Sipp front cover, 17(b), 18; Tom Walker 4, 21(c); Alain Rainon 5(c), 9; Sylvain Cordier 7; Jean-Philippe Varin 12(b); Éric A. Soder 16(t); Éric Dragesco 21(t). Sunset: Alaska Stock title page, 6, 21(b); Gérard Lacz 2, 8, 13(b), 14, 15, 20, 22-23; S. Camazine 12(t); N.H.P.A. 13(t); Animals 17(t).

English translation: Deirdre Halat
Gareth Stevens editor: Barbara Kiely Miller
Gareth Stevens art direction: Tammy West
Gareth Stevens designer: Kami Strunsee

Printed in the United States of America

1 2 3 4 5 6 7 8 9 10 09 08 07 06